* A PARODY *

THE RABBIT WHO WANTS TO GO TO HARVARD

BY ZELDAR THE GREAT

IN CONJUNCTION WITH QUICK-FIX PUBLISHING

WITH HELP FROM DIANA HOLQUIST AND CHRISTOPHER ELIOPOULOS

DIAL BOOKS

To desperate parents everywhere who want to **buy this book**, now
[get out your wallet]. You, ***[name]***, cannot resist.
You are just now buying this book . . .
—Z. the G.

For my brilliant kids, who now *really* don't have a shot at Harvard.
Sorry, guys.
—D.H.

For my sister, Marian
—C.E.

DIAL BOOKS • Penguin Young Readers Group
An imprint of Penguin Random House LLC • 375 Hudson Street, New York, NY 10014

Text copyright © 2015 by Diana Holquist • Pictures copyright © 2015 by Christopher Eliopoulos

ISBN: 978-0-399-53928-2

Printed in the United States of America
1 3 5 7 9 10 8 6 4 2
Designed by Jason Henry • Text set in Napoleone Slab ITC
The artwork for this book was created digitally.

INSTRUCTIONS TO THE READER

WARNING! Never read this book out loud to any child who will be competing for your child's spot at Harvard (without following the instruction below). The author and publisher take no responsibility when your child ends up in therapy.

The Rabbit Who Wants to Go to Harvard uses powerful psychological methods designed to make small children do what you want, when you want. These powerful methods give suggestions to the child's unconscious mind. It is recommended that you read the story from beginning to end, even if that is excruciatingly unbearable for everyone involved. This book must be read correctly for guaranteed admission to Harvard:

- **Bold text** means you should read in a louder voice than normal.
- *Italic text* means you should read in a slow and soothing voice.
- ***Bold italic text*** means you should read fast and loud and slow and calm ***all at the same time***.
- ***BOLD ITALIC ALL-CAPS TEXT*** means all bets are off. Run!
- Sometimes, you are asked to make a scary face or dance the Macarena. These parts are marked as ***[action]***. Other parts of the book indicate ***[name]*** where you should insert your child's name.
- You can substitute "Stanford" or "MIT" for "Harvard" depending on the most recent *U.S. News & World Report* college rankings.
- When reading this book to your insufferable, I-*devoured*-Proust-in-the-original-French-at-two-years-old niece, ***[pretentious name]***, who **will** take *your child's* spot at Harvard because her dad is a loaded Harvard alumnus and you went to *state school* ***[shiver]***, no worries. Just substitute "local community college" for "Harvard." Or, for more delightful results, **pick up a copy of** the extremely effective ***The Rabbit Who Wants to Work at Denny's***. And the audiobook. **Now.**

Be well and *keep dreaming!*

Zeldar the Great

HYPNOTIST, ACADEMIC ADVISOR, AND BESTSELLING AUTHOR

I am going to tell you a story that will make you feel too anxious to sleep. Now, some people get anxious straightaway whilst others sleep a little while first. But you and I both know, *[name]*, that **sleep is for losers**. You'll have plenty of time to **sleep when you're dead**. So I'm wondering just when will be the best time for you, *[name]*, to **wake the heck up and start working to get your sleepy little *[age]*-year-old butt into Harvard,** now or before the story ends...

O nce upon a time, there was a rabbit called Ronald who really wanted to fall asleep, and could **not, right now**. Because his mother had other ideas. His mother was obsessed with *Harvard*.

Ronald was very little. He did not know what Harvard was. This made him nervous. *Very, very nervous. Now.* Other toddlers know what Harvard is, Ronald. They have already started their neurobiology tutoring. **Stay on your toes, little rabbit! Life is not one big cozy naptime.**

Ronald the Rabbit is just your age, *[name]*. Not older nor younger, but exactly your age, *[name]*. In other words, you and Ronald the Rabbit are in competition. You and **EVERYONE** are in competition. Harvard only has 2,081 slots. Do you know how quickly rabbits reproduce? There are oceans of those guys out there, *piles of rabbits*, gunning for your spot at Harvard.

All of Ronald's siblings easily fell asleep every evening, so don't worry about those slacker lagomorphs *[whip out chart of rabbit taxonomic orders and have child memorize]*. Worry about Ronald. He was wide-awake, thinking of all the things he would do to **get into Harvard, now.** He could **study** for his SATs, and **practice** his violin, and do his French conjugations, and **set up meetings** for the seed funding of his biotech start-up...

He was about to **get up,** he did not know how soon. **Now.** How **close to achieving** he really is. How the picture of him and you, *[name],* achieving becomes clearer and closer with every breath, **now.** In this in-between place, right before achieving, I control your mind. You, *[name],* will do what I say. You, *[name],* will obey.

You, *[name],* will go to Harvard.

Tonight, Ronald's siblings fell asleep faster than usual *[make L shape with thumb and forefinger and hold up to forehead]*, whilst Ronald was lying there **thinking** about all the things that can make him **smarter now**. *All the studying, all the cramming, and all the other things that would cause him to get into Harvard, right now.*

But could he do even more?

Ronald the Rabbit was a bit of a bootlicker, so he decided to ask his mommy. Mommy Rabbit was in her bedroom, on her treadmill, scouring the CollegeConfidential.com forums on her phone even though it was three a.m. She said that Ronald should *take all the thoughts that were lingering in his head about sleep, fun, and other kid stuff* and **put them in a box** by the bed.

Ronald said, "Even my very favorite *Peter Rabbit* book?"

Mommy Rabbit said, "Yes, especially *Peter Rabbit*. Peter Rabbit is a thief. He would not **get into Harvard.**"

Mommy Rabbit took a gulp of her "coffee" and continued: "Tomorrow when you wake up, I will have crushed all those childish desires and you will forget about them." Mommy Rabbit said this with **certainty** in her voice and **vodka** on her breath. "You will **forget the joys** you put in your box."

Ronald filled the box. It felt *very relaxing to free his mind* and do as Mommy Rabbit said so that she would not freak out and give Ronald the silent treatment.

Ronald is now ready to **get into Harvard.**

Mommy Rabbit said it was time to see Admission Officer Owl, who lived just on the other side of the Charles River, in Cambridge. Cambridge is very lovely. Mommy Rabbit very badly wants to go there on parents' weekend for brunch in her Harvard sweatshirt and new Tory Burch flats. *She'd have a Bloody Mary, alone, because where would Daddy Rabbit be that weekend? Working again! He didn't know how hard it was to be alone with children all day and half the night, pushing them to study and play their instruments.* **[Pour another drink.]** *He can go to hell.*

After Ronald and Mommy Rabbit had walked for a while, they met Adderall Aardvark.

"Where are you off to?" asked Adderall Aardvark wolfishly.

"I am going to visit Admission Officer Owl," said Ronald the Rabbit. "He will help me **get into Harvard**. Do you know how to **get into Harvard?**" asked Ronald.

Adderall Aardvark held out his hand. He was holding something.

"This always works for me," said Adderall Aardvark.

"Thank you, I will try it," said Ronald the Rabbit.

Adderal Aardvark said, **"You will get into Harvard. Now. Allow yourself to get into Harvard."**

Ronald and Mommy Rabbit left Adderall Aardvark. Now Ronald took giant steps, crooked hops, and twirling spins. *He felt more awake. He felt how invigorating it was when he did exactly what his mommy said.*

For a while. Then the nausea set in.

"Mommy, can we sit down and read the bunny book about the garden and Mr. McGregor like we used to?" asked Ronald the Rabbit.

"Ronald, those days are past. Reading is for parental mind control now. Reading must get **results. Now.** Please keep walking. This will all be over soon."

But not soon enough. You, *[name]*, are less than halfway through this book. How is that possible? *You, [name], feel you cannot make it. But you can. You must. Keep reading. If you can't get through this simple children's book, how will you, [name], ever get through Harvard?*

After a while Ronald and Mommy Rabbit met the beautiful and wise Kollege Koach Kitty. She sat on a huge pile of cash next to the path.

"Hello, Kollege Koach Kitty. Since you're a wise kitty, I would like your help to **get into Harvard.** Can you help me?" asked Ronald.

"Of course I can help you to **get into Harvard**," answered the wise kitty. "It will cost you four thousand dollars. Cash."

Mommy Rabbit handed over the bills. *[Pour another drink.]*

"I want you to **focus** on different parts of your application. **It's important that you do as I tell you**," the kitty said.

Since Kollege Koach Kitty is wise, I will do what she tells me, thought Ronald.

"Join a varsity sports team." Ronald did as Kitty told him.

"Take up an orchestral instrument." Ronald did so **now.**

"Publish a scientific paper in a nationally recognized journal." Ronald did so, **now.**

"Don't **worry** about your essays, Ronald. I will write those," said Kitty.

"I can write them," Ronald said. "I want to study literature and write real children's books full of fun and imagination."

Kollege Koach Kitty hissed and bopped Ronald on the head *[tap child's head firmly]*.

"Take your SATs," Kitty said. Ronald did so, now. And **again and again and again,** trying to land those last ten points. Ronald was **getting close. Now.**

Then Kollege Koach Kitty said, "It is time. Turn in your application. Hit the send button and it will fly *down, down, down*. Just like a leaf that falls *slowly down, down, down, slowly down* from a tree."

Ronald hit send. What a relief! All at once, Ronald felt *how tired he had become from his soccer tournaments, chamber concerts, charity galas, all-nighters in the bio lab, and his intense SAT prep. Ronald hadn't slept in fourteen years. But it was all worth it.*

Good bunny!

Ronald worked hard just like **you, [name], will work hard. You, [name], will work even harder than Ronald.** You, *[name]*, might even have to trip him up a little if you can't get those last ten points on your SAT. **You, [name], must start working harder. Now.**

Soon it will be time to rest.

But not yet.

After walking for a while, Ronald and Mommy Rabbit reached Admission Officer Owl's office. Outside the building there was a big sign that read **"I can make anyone get into Harvard."**

There was a line outside of 34,295 rabbits, plus their mommies, and their college coaches and behavioral therapists too.

Ronald and Mommy Rabbit finally reached the door. There was another sign. It read "Knock on the door **now, when you are ready to go to Harvard.**" Ronald decided that **he was ready to go to Harvard, now.** He knocked on the door.

Admission Officer Owl opened the door and was happy to see Ronald and Mommy Rabbit. Only not so much Mommy Rabbit. The owl tried to avoid mommy rabbits, especially ones with buggy eyes who smell like vodka. They gave him the heebie-jeebies.

Also, the situation was difficult overall, as owls like very much to eat rabbits.

"Welcome, my friends," said Admission Officer Owl. "Apparently, you would like some help to **get into Harvard, now.**"

Admission Officer Owl held up his **powerful, magical, sparkly admission powder** that makes rabbits and children get into Harvard when it is sprinkled over them.

"I will now read this spell and sprinkle the admission powder over you. This spell is powerful and always works. **You will get into Harvard, now.**

"Are you a first-generation college student?" asked Admission Officer Owl.

"No," said Ronald Rabbit.

The owl did not sprinkle the admission powder over Ronald.

Mommy Rabbit frowned.

"Are you related to powerful, wealthy alumni?" asked the owl.

"No," said Ronald.

"Are you from Alaska?" asked the owl.

"No," said Ronald.

"Shame," said Owl. "Are you a world-class athlete?"

"No."

"Tuba player?"

"No."

"Ronald, what have you got? Why should I sprinkle admission powder on your head?"

"*I took eleven APs, have excellent extra-curriculars with tons of leadership positions, near-perfect SATs, and a 3.99 unweighted GPA.*"

Owl yawned.

Ronald leaned in close. He whispered so that Mommy Rabbit couldn't hear. "Look, Mr. Owl, I got a five on my chemistry AP. I don't believe in magic powder. You are holding up tiny plastic particles coated with titanium dioxide commonly known as glitter. Mr. Owl, my mommy might be gullible—hey, she bought this book, didn't she?—but don't mess with *me*."

The owl opened his eyes wide. "*But*—magic—**powerful psychological methods**—!"

"Mr. Owl, I want to go to Harvard to learn about literature," Ronald said. "I want to learn how to write books like *Peter Rabbit*, even though no one reads them anymore because they're too busy with this *magic* crap."

Admission Officer Owl said in a quiet voice so that Mommy Rabbit couldn't hear, "If you go to Harvard, do you promise to **write a real children's book about me? Get me out of this mind-control rabbit hell hole? And rescue Kitty and Aardvark, too?**"

"Yes," Ronald said. "Just don't tell Mommy. She wants me to be a thoracic surgeon bunny."

"But wait—isn't she the one reading this to you?"

"No. She bought me the audiobook *[buy the audiobook now for only $9.99]*. She set it on an infinite loop so she can sit in the corner checking her iPhone and fuming about how I got that B+ in gym. She's not really paying attention."

They both looked over at Mommy Rabbit. It was true.

"Good bunny," said Admission Officer Owl. "Now go home and wait for your admission email. No promises—the 3.99 hurts. But I will see what I can do."

Ronald and Mommy Rabbit thanked the owl and walked home.

After a while, they met the beautiful and wise Kollege Koach Kitty. Kitty told Ronald, "I can tell that you are **very close to getting into Harvard, now.**" She winked at him. "I got a text from Owl."

Ronald was very tired. He slowly nodded his head. He whispered, *"I will write my children's book and make you a **beautiful** kitty, with **charm** and a **much less depressing** job."*

Kitty purred. "In my seventh life, I was a poet."

Ronald continued home. He was *more tired with every step.*

What was all that noise? What was happening?

Adderall Aardvark was getting arrested by the cops. **"Hey, I went to Harvard,"** said Adderall Aardvark to the police officer. **"You can't treat me like this."**

Ronald the Rabbit was now so tired he could barely lift his feet. But still Ronald and Mommy Rabbit continued home to wait for the owl's email.

When Ronald got home, he tried to **stay awake.** But he was so, so tired.

The computer dinged.

Ronald Rabbit had mail!

Ronald Rabbit opened the email.

He did not **get into Harvard.**

He was rejected.

At first, he was very sad.

But then, he had an idea.

He went into Mommy Rabbit's room. He opened the box. He got out all the playthings that had been shut away for so long. He got out his crayons. He sat down on the floor and he wrote a children's book. Owl was there, and Kitty and Aardvark. The book had no repetitive sentences, italics, or bolded type. It was not **scientific** or **powerful.** It was just **absolutely, fantastically wonderful.** He put the story into an envelope and he sent it to Harvard.

Harvard sent him a second email . . . ding!

Ronald jolted awake. It was four a.m. Mommy was in his room. He was confused. Had the owl's email come? Had he really broken into the box? Or was it all a dream?

"Did I get in, Mommy?" Ronald asked. "What did the email say? How does the story end?"

Mommy Rabbit looked up from the book she was reading. "Yes, Ronald. The email came. **YOU GOT INTO HARVARD!** But you fell asleep before I could tell you."

Ronald was so happy. I can read *Peter Rabbit* now, thought Ronald. I can read it every night! For the rest of my life! *Mommy Rabbit will finally leave me alone and stop thinking that it's her job to micromanage my every move. She will back off. She will trust me to find my own calm, contented place.*

Mommy Rabbit held up the book in her hand. "I got you this present, Ronald. I will read it to you now. It is called *The Rabbit Who Wants to Go to Stanford Medical School.*" *[Buy it now for $15.99.]* She took a sip of her "coffee," and she started to read.

The Rabbit Who Wants to Go to Stanford Medical School, the next title in the Quick-Fix series, is available now wherever books and pharmaceuticals are sold.

ABOUT THE AUTHOR AND ILLUSTRATOR

DIANA HOLQUIST (Dianaholquist.com) is the author of several romance novels, including those published as Sophie Gunn, as well as the parenting memoir *Battle Hymn of the Tiger Daughter*. A graduate of Columbia University and former advertising copywriter, she lives near Philadelphia, Pennsylvania, with her husband, two teenagers, and three cats.

CHRISTOPHER ELIOPOULOS (Chriseliopoulos.com) began his illustration career as a letterer for Marvel, and has worked on thousands of comics. He is also the illustrator of the *New York Times* bestselling Ordinary People Change the World series written by Brad Meltzer. He lives in Northern New Jersey with his wife and their identical twin sons.